BY THE AUTHOR OF THE GREAT C

YOU GET

20 PRACTICAL AND EMOTIONAL LESSONS

THE AGENCY

TO MAXIMIZE YOUR AGENCY

YOU DESERVE

AND PARTNER RELATIONSHIP

BY JARED BELSKY

First printing 2023

Book cover designed by Andrew Vogel
Illustrations designed by Emma Brown
Book interior designed by Andrew Vogel

ISBN 979-8-9882706-0-7 Paperback
ISBN 979-8-9882706-1-4 Hardback
ISBN 979-8-9882706-2-1 E-book

Published by Ripples Media
www.ripples.media

DEDICATION

To my family who makes life interesting, loving, and fun.
To all the incredible clients I have had the privilege to
work with over the years.

CONTENTS

INTRODUCTION

There are millions of people out there who manage the relationships between their companies and the agencies and consultancies they've hired. However, there is very little conversation that centers around how to foster great relationships that in turn generate maximum value. By asking how to ensure you are a great client, the relationship will grow along with your results. Yet, so few pause to ask how to be the best possible client. Why is this?

The reasons for this are threefold. First, leaders on the client side are rarely, if ever, forced to be great clients because of a complicated power dynamic. Secondly, there is little to no coaching or information on *how* to be a great client. Lastly, marketing executives too often don't understand or internalize why it's worth the extra effort to be a great client versus a good client. Don't get me wrong, there are scores of great clients, and much of this book is dedicated to celebrating the great ones. I am merely suggesting they are less common than they could be if there were more understanding of all the trapped potential. If you searched Amazon for "books about being a great client" you will find zero books, which surprised me but also furthered my pursuit to fill this information void. What if those people hiring and managing agencies were more curious as to how to be the *best* possible client and reap the rewards of that excellence? What if there were some practical ways to help them?

When you join a new company, you typically spend days or weeks learning norms, people, rules, processes, and procedures. The idea of course is that preparation leads to success. For example, when I joined the Coca-Cola Company, they were highly invested in my onboarding in almost every sense. Their onboarding was truly incredible, and I still have many great memories and friends from my time there. I learned the core values. I learned how to use their many systems to pull data on sales trends, and I was trained in how to participate in the many HR and developmental systems and programs.

Though it was a top-notch onboarding experience at Coca-Cola, I recall one notable gap. I was the media steward for the Fanta brand and in charge of a budget that was several million dollars at the time. Specifically, I was put in charge of maximizing the value of working with our media agency. I certainly was trained on our target audience, our goals, and so many other things, but I was not trained in how to manage that agency relationship itself.

On the agency side, there was a team of five to ten people tasked with helping Fanta plan, buy, and measure our media, and ultimately invest the millions of dollars we were budgeted to spend. Perhaps I was supposed to have relied on common sense. Perhaps the agency should have known how to manage itself. In the end, I relied on instinct and did my best (which was not that great).

With the benefit of hindsight and a lot of reflection, it's clear there should be extensive training on managing the relationships between your partners and agencies just as you have training on anything else involving a big expense and a critical outcome. Since that experience, I have realized that Coca-Cola is not unique in this opportunity gap. This notion of training on how to be a great client is something that just does not exist. It does not exist in the Fortune 500, nor does it exist in the mid-market or the SMB market. It is not common anywhere.

Over the past few years, I have asked over one hundred marketing heads, CMOs, CEOs, and various business leaders one very simple question: *Did you ever train on how to be an effective client for an agency or services partner?* I chose this question because it provided no space to hide. This question was purposely worded not to judge their intention (i.e., *Do you care about your agency and consultancy partners?*), but to honestly ask them just that. The question is also powerful because it provides a lot of room for introspection.

Just about every colleague replied, after a pause, with some version of "nope, I did not." After contemplating my question, sometimes staring awkwardly into space, similar versions of these three answers kept getting repeated.

First, they were never mandated to be great at managing agencies.

In other words, regarding their own goals or KPIs (Key Performance Indicators), not once had their boss evaluated them on how they handled their agency relationships. If the old adage is true that "people respect what you inspect," there was little to no inspection in this area. Therefore, there was little to no incentive to improve if the manager was not watching or expecting them to focus on nurturing these relationships.

Second, they never were trained in how to be great at the art and science of managing an agency.

Literally, not a single person in over a hundred interviews shared that there was dedicated training regarding how to manage this sort of relationship investment. Think about how profound that is for a second. The vast majority of Fortune 500 companies have media or creative or consulting agencies with annual retainers that can be as large as $30 million per year in fees, with as much as $1 billion in media investment under management. Yet leaders are asked to sort of "wing it" in the management and stewardship of that investment. I would challenge you to think of an equivalent.

Third, which was the most honest and telling answer, they felt there were "zero repercussions to *not* being great."

The C-Suite in certain situations can be shortsighted with agency dynamics because it is easier to fire an agency than deal with their routines and processes that might be broken or need significant improvement. It's easier to hire a new agency than address their product issues. In short, not being great at managing the relationship with your agency partner was not viewed as a failure in the hallways of most companies, even if and when you actually fail your agency. Instead, it gets spun as though the agency is always to blame, and so, you run yet another RFP (Request For Proposal).

I was curious to see if this was the norm across the board or just the consensus of my own sample set of CMO friends. As a result, I commissioned an additional survey of 300 client-side individuals. From their responses, this was the norm in all of their respective companies. Additionally, 86% were interested in learning how to be a better client.

Further, I began speaking with several agency owners I know in media, creative, and analytics and I posed the same questions to them, only to hear similar responses, but from the other side. Interestingly, most agencies invested very little time in training clients to be ideal clients. Sure, agencies created briefs and conducted onboarding rituals, but those are very different from finding real ways and processes for clients to perform their best to serve everyone's collective mutual interests.

So, what does make for a great client since we have established that the industry does not incentivize people to step up and focus on this issue?

At the end of the day, a great client is able to motivate, to be firm but fair, to share information freely and generously, and to work to lower the temperature when things go wrong. Navigating those moments are what defines your ability around agency management. A great client believes in partnership. Partnership, as much as anything, means sharing and having the long view. Sharing generously comes in the form of sharing data, sharing information, sharing specific briefs, and always working toward a feeling that there is one team. The long view comes into play because, just like an internal marketing team, there are good days and bad days. Good months and bad months. A great client understands and is willing to look at the client-agency relationship in a longitudinal manner looking to understand if things are getting better over time.

Too many clients believe those tough moments are solely the duty of the agency to sort through. The average client-agency tenure is sitting at just under two years. This data point is wilder when you realize that some RFP processes take three to six months. When there are tough moments, the best clients go into a "coach first" mentality and are willing to treat you as though you are part of their team. They dig in and try to help set the right course.

If you picked up this book, you are already ahead of the curve. It means you want to be the best. It means you believe that if you can be an inspirational client for your agency, it will not only help them but in turn help you.

My sincere hope is that this very practical, easy-to-read book will provide a few critical pointers for client-side folks to be able to have more successful and productive relationships with their clients. It does not need to be read in full. It is meant to be a usable, practical guide to making you the best possible client, so that you can in turn get more out of your agencies.

Section 1
TEN PRACTICAL LESSONS

For this first section, let's focus on the practical ways to be the best client to your agency and service providers. We will start with the early phase of the relationship and learn how to navigate a better RFP process, a great onboarding, and how to ensure those Master Service Agreements/ Statements of Work (MSA/SOW) negotiations don't come back to haunt your relationship later. From there, we'll add the techniques that will ensure you provide your partner with the right guideposts and signals to help them be as productive as possible. This will include tools regarding creating and presenting great briefings, how to get on the same page about the company's goals for the work product, and so on. The focus next turns to learning how to navigate bumpy waters so that you can get through the inevitable tough times with your agency partner.

Your agency partners will love and respect you even more for strategizing and considering both parties in this relationship.

CHAPTER 1

Dump the Normal RFP Process and Consider an Alternative

Every day, clients are contemplating or getting ready to issue an RFP to an agency or service provider.

I would argue that too often, an agency search is a referendum on skills, tools, and technologies when instead it should be an exploration of DNA and core value alignment. Whether you are looking for a creative, tech, media, analytics, or UX agency, there tend to be many partner options where the true skill set may be within a 20% variance. However, the culture, the DNA, the process, the transparency, the team, and the ability to listen to feedback and take direction, well, that part tends to be something that clients should allocate more time and inspection towards.

My longtime friend Carrie Schonberg, the current CMO of the number one private homebuilder Ashton Woods, has used the following lens to find agencies that she can stay with for often a decade at a time. Carrie shared, "My agencies are an extension of my team. When we do an RFP, it's a very thoughtful and intentional process. We don't just look at the *what* (the skills), but we focus tremendously on the *who*. The *who* means that the agency prospect has culture and core values that align with that of our team and our companies. We look for agencies that can and will take feedback well, be curious, and keep evolving with us. I am looking for an agency team who individually and collectively feels personally invested in our success and view it as their success as well."

To build on Carrie's invaluable advice, I would recommend you focus on the following four things when trying to search for a new agency partner:

Understand what the leadership of the agency is about and stands for — Since agencies are 100% people-based businesses, the agencies tend to take on a certain amount of traits inherited from the leadership team. These people tend to be fairly public with their speaking engagements, awards, articles, and blog posts. A few things you may want to jot down and look for:

• It is not hard to discover if the leadership team is flashy and loud, or quiet and humble. Flashy and loud might mean more focus goes into "the show" when you want more focus on the work.

• Has the leadership team been together for a few

years creating stability, or is it a revolving door? If the top of the agency is a revolving door, then the rest of the agency will also be a revolving door.

• Are the agency leads "panel people" jetting around from CES to Cannes to SXSW, or are they grinding behind the scenes working on your issues and coaching up the team?

• Can you ask for a reference about leadership involvement? Are they hands on? Or are they "a glass of wine and golf" people? If you ask specifically for references around leadership's involvement, will you get silence?

Understand the Core Values of the agency and how they are presented on a Tuesday at 2 p.m. when nobody is watching — All agencies have core values. Many times, the average employee can't recite them. In other cases, the core values are central to the agency and are lived out, especially when no executive is watching on a Tuesday at 2 p.m. Do your best to discover what the core values are and more importantly if and how they are practiced.

• Consider creating a step in the process for the core team to share agency core values and what they mean to each team member. Ask for specific examples.

• Consider asking for evidence of what this looks

like on a "Tuesday at 2 p.m." You will learn a ton just by seeing what they bring and share to that show-and-tell.

•   Consider asking when and how the agency held on to its core values during a time of tumult and strain, because core values are often most in jeopardy when times are tough.

Get clarity on who the "real team" is going to be — During pitches, you tend to meet the best of the best. You tend to meet the Head of Strategy and the Head of Media. People with fancy ascots, great presentation skills, and jokes timed to the second … all of which have been informally or not, focus grouped to the choreography level of a Broadway show. In many cases, those people will never see you again. What is critical is that you ask to meet with at least the day-to-day account person, strategist, analyst, and creative person. Ask "who will I be talking to at least 50% of the time each week?" And then, make sure you meet them. And then, request they put that in the contract!

To be fair, a great agency does not have people just sitting around doing nothing. So, be creative and patient in the way that the agency may share these names and people as likely there are rotations and/or hiring that have to occur. Additionally, budget is a factor. The larger the remit, the more you can ask in terms of team construction. Like most of this book goes on to preach, I am just suggesting two-way fairness.

Creating an opportunity for problem-solving in real time is better than drawn-out cases — Test case studies, commonly given out during RFP processes to select an agency, do not actually reveal what the client wants to learn. When an agency is given a test case study, and subsequently given two weeks, they can put ten, twenty, or thirty employees or FTEs (Full-Time Equivalents) on the case behind the scenes. Frankly, half the time the agency brings in freelancers who don't even draw a W2 from that agency. In short, the perfect case answer you get delivered is sort of like ordering through a drive-thru window and not knowing who the actual chef is or where the food comes from. Instead, focus on doing more joint problem-solving and spontaneous Q&A. This lets you see what your core and eventual team is actually made of.

In an ideal scenario, you are trying to solve for:
- critical problem-solving
- the ability to actively listen
- ideation ability
- the ability to take feedback and collaborate

In all my years on the agency side, I have only seen this done expertly once. I was involved in an RFP for Pernod Ricard, a major global spirits brand. It was

Round Three in the process, which was the "case study" round. Instead of the usual theater, we were instead told we would host the client in our collaboration room for a full-day exercise. Together, we would work a problem.

As we entered the room, the agency was given a marketing task. "If the goal of this particular vodka is to 'own the night,' what would you do to solve that problem with our target audience?" We then worked on the problem together with the client, sharing our insights and hypotheses, hearing feedback from our prospective clients, and then pivoting based on that direction, and finally sharing some ideas. This allowed them in real-time to ascertain if we were A) good listeners and B) collaborative. I credit Andre and Tim with this forward-thinking idea. It ended up setting the tone for a great and trusting relationship.

Be bold and re-think the RFP process. *Adage* recently reported that 40% of clients are searching for a new agency. So, if almost half the time people are looking for a new partner, it suggests the selection process is what is broken. I would encourage you to look at the real team, real problem solving, leadership culture, and agency's core values as the picture suggests on the following page.

Your goal as the client should be to build and evaluate a "house of trust" during this RFP cycle, not just an IRS-like evaluation of tools and tech. Ask yourself, what will the house you co-build with your new agency partner look and feel like?

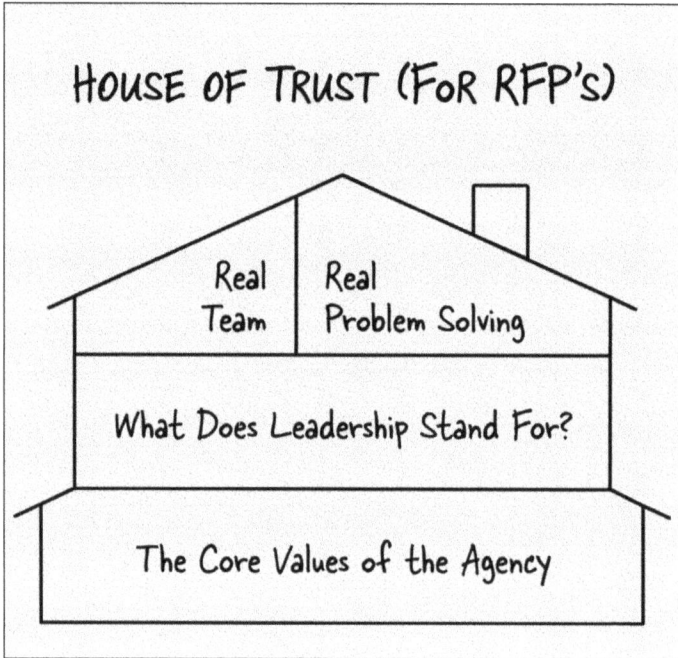

HOUSE OF TRUST (FoR RFP's)

Real Team

Real Problem Solving

What Does Leadership Stand For?

The Core Values of the Agency

CHAPTER 2

How to Create a Good Honeymoon Phase When Hiring an Agency

So, you picked your partner in some sort of process that had you evaluate Agency A over Agencies B, C, and D. You are very pleased with your choice and have the highest of hopes for what you will accomplish together. What too often happens next is that the new partner is slammed into the thick of things, without being set up for success. They are rushed into creating dashboards, getting ready for a shoot next week, or working in the engines and auctions to find the 20% growth you need to show your boss or board ASAP.

I get it, you are under major pressure to grow. However, if your urgency and pressure sour the start of what could be a very large investment, it will not help you in the long run. If you can set up your partner for success with a bit of planning, it will pay dividends.

The agency partner needs an opportunity to be onboarded *and* to onboard you. Yes, that is not a typo, there are two types of onboardings. Too often in our industry, both get skipped in the name of speed.

The client needs to onboard the agency. This allows the agency to truly understand the client.

You should prepare to invest at least three to four weeks in onboarding the agency partner. This should consist of at least six core activities.

1. Culture and Values — Take the time to share with the agency partner your core values. How did they come to be? Why are they so important? How are they used and exhibited by employees at the company? How is the agency expected to carry out those core values? How does your CEO talk about your unique company DNA? Which stories stand out as uniquely representative of your culture at its best?

2. Historical work — Take out examples of past work, media plans, tests, briefs, decks, and whatever else you can find. Put them on a wall (digital or analog) and share what was positive and negative about those experiences. History will repeat itself unless you take the time to not allow it to happen.

3. Do a store walk with your team — One of my favorite clients took the time to invite our team members down to their core market and do a proper tour of the stores. They offered to do this on their own time, making a point to let the agency team know how important the understanding of those stores and guest behavior was to them.

4. Economics of the business — Take the time to help your agency understand how the business model works. If you are Kraft Cheese, the agency has to understand that all the great creative in the world is no match for a 30% increase in core ingredients and related cost of goods sold (COGS). If you are a credit card company, help your agency understand how underwriting and credit risk management works and how that in turn changes marketing.

I was so grateful when the CMO and president of Red Roof Inn took the time to help me understand their business model, the mindset of the hotel operators, and a deep dive into understanding how allowing pets to stay free was a core proposition. Don't skip this step.

5. Goals for the year — Review in depth what your goals are for the year. Consider sharing three sets of goals:

A. *Company Goals* — At the company level, what are the CEO and Board of Directors working to achieve?

B. *Division/Product Goals* — At the division or product level, what are the KPIs?

C. *Your Personal Goals* — Third, but surely not least, is the importance of sharing YOUR goals. When an agency understands the goals assigned to the client, that vulnerability in turn unleashes huge empathy and understanding.

6. Executive point of view — A really important, and often missed opportunity, is to have the most senior applicable executive speak to the entire agency team. This might be the CMO or the CEO depending on the remit of the agency or services partner. Ideally, this person would dedicate a proper one to two hours to meet everyone on the agency team from the most senior person to the most junior analyst or copywriter. This senior leader ideally speaks to three things:

  A. *The importance of the relationship*
  B. *The importance of what the company does*
  C. *The importance of the moment*

The agency needs the chance to onboard as well!

This should consist of at least four core activities on their side:

1. Explanation of team roles and responsibilities — Demand that the agency does not shortcut the phase where it should explain what each person does on the team, and how you will interface with that person.

2. Explanation of the briefing process — Ask the agency to share their briefing templates. Spend the time to customize those now, when things are calm, before the storm. A brief can take a number of forms. Co-create one that will work for this new relationship. The process for creating a great all-purpose brief will also be discussed in the next chapter.

3. **Calendar ritual expectation setting** — Every agency has some sort of "calendar" of rituals. When are agency/client check-ins? When are weekly reports best shared? When are the intra-agency huddles? How long does the client need to gain creative approvals for their boss?

4. **Reporting, KPI alignment, and understanding** — The agency should explain very clearly its reporting rituals. Whether these are performance, accounting, quarterly business reviews (QBRs), or wrap reports, each agency has ideal timing, templates, and so forth. This is a chance to not only understand these artifacts, but also have them mold a bit to your calendar.

(Pro tip—if your CFO, for example, is looking for performance metrics every Friday, you will want reporting to come from your agency on a Thursday to give you time to listen, ingest, and then incorporate.)

When this ideal onboarding is given the necessary time during this needed honeymoon phase, client-agency relationships are given their best shot. There is a reason why marriages start with a honeymoon trip. The trip allows the young couple to bond, relax, and get to know each other in an idyllic environment before the realities of marriage set in so that they have that reservoir of goodwill toward each other. This is the same for client and agency life. I know how busy you are, and how tempting it is to slam your agency into a brief, but please use the first two to three weeks for a proper **mutual** onboarding and honeymoon phase!

CHAPTER 3

The Core Ingredients of a Great All-Purpose Brief

A great brief is a tool clients can use to synthesize their challenges and distill them into a short (one-to-three page) document that gives your partner agency all it needs to know about the challenge to go and create magic.

There are scores of acceptable formats for a great brief, and they all must be tailored. They will also vary tremendously based on whether it's a creative-focused brief, a media-focused brief, an analytics-focused brief, a design-focused brief, or something entirely different.

The core ingredients of any great brief are all the same and yet are too often forgotten or missed. The core ingredients help an agency or partner really understand the true *why*. The intention here is to help you take a step in the right direction. I am not a strategist by trade, and I will be the first to tell you I am no briefing master. I have seen over the years that there are a few core questions that should be part of any world-class brief, so that if and when your partner forgets to ask these questions, go ahead and push them forward with the help of some of the below:

1. Why are we marketing in the first place?

There are one hundred things you could do with your money. Take a step back to answer this question. Yeah, it's a tough question, but one that needs answering.

2. Who are we talking to?

Yes, we want to see your trove of audience research, but we also want to see you take one bold line and distill down who the target is in a very meaningful and brief way. Use this challenge to make choices. Choice makes your results, and our work, better and stronger.

3. What is your right to win?

What is your way to winning? Why now? Why are you better? Why does the world need you/this now? A right to win must be bold and clear.

4. What is the key message?

You should share the main message you want your project to communicate to your target audience. What problem does your product solve? What's the angle for your campaign? How will you get your message across? What is most important to showcase?

5. What are we making and what deliverables should be provided?

You might not feel like you know the full answer,

but it's interesting to share what you think initially as a way to guide your agency partner. Describe what the end result looks like. The agency has delivered the following X things and we are high-fiving as a result of it.

6. What measurement hurdles have existed in the past that you want to remedy?

Spell out the historical data blockers that have previously existed, and give recommendations to your agency on how they can help you assess metrics.

7. What is the tone and spirit of what we are making and what is the voice like?

Every brand, campaign, and project has a tone. Is it lively? Is it tranquil? Is it playful? Is it serious or informative?

8. What are your wildest wishes and ideas?

This is your dream moment in the brief. Pretend your agency is a magic genie, what can they make come true for you?

9. Where could you get stuck?

Be half-empty for a minute. Where could the agency get stuck? How can you help them anticipate these potholes in advance?

10. How will you measure success?

This is where you state very clearly a *singular* goal you will judge this entire work-stream around. It will be very tempting to write brand awareness, sales, consideration, loyalty, retention, and world peace.

Come on…admit it…*you have done that before, haven't you?* Well, avoid it. The best briefs have one singular goal in mind. When Apple famously launched its 1984 ad, it was to create awareness for this new Mac and the related revolution.

11. If you landed from Mars and knew nothing about us, our politics, or our feelings, what are three things about us that make no sense?

Play the contrarian role and pick the idea apart. Sharpen the brief by attempting to poke holes in all of the previous points and messaging.

So, now you know the right questions to ask and answer to help guide your agency partner. Perhaps, the remaining question is **when?**

Too often, clients only deploy a brief for a big new campaign or the kick-off of a fresh planning cycle. I would instead coach you to believe that a brief can be used not just for big and special occasions, but also for basic needs that should be clarified. Just like in your interpersonal relationships, mind-reading rarely, if ever, goes well. Help your partner to their best odds of success by taking the sixty minutes required to fill out something like the above for any project that is beyond the standard day-to-day. You will be a client hero for it.

CHAPTER 4

How a Bad MSA/SOW Can Hurt You More than You Realize

So…you are very excited that you picked your agency or services firm of choice. You feel total excitement, hope, and energy wondering what type of results and expertise they will bring to your world.

Then, you ruin it all with a terrible MSA/SOW (Master Service Agreement/ Statement of Work) negotiation and tarnish the goodwill created during the courtship process. Far more than goodwill is destroyed. What most clients don't realize is that a lot of downstream challenges happen when there is a poor MSA/SOW negotiation. Clients don't realize this because often they don't see the middle part of negotiations. Typically, a senior client is very involved in the selection and pitch phase of finding a new agency. Then, there is this handoff moment where procurement gets involved or maybe some other third party like a general counsel. In this stage, too often changes are made to the scope or MSA in the name of some mandate. During this phase, changes to staffing, economics, and various other rules come back to bite agencies and clients alike.

Furthermore, a lot of clients or procurement teams "win" the MSA/SOW battle only to lose the eventual quality war. This is not intentional, but rather an accidental byproduct when the interests of the marketing and procurement teams aren't aligned.

The procurement team is often incentivized to get the most advantageous pricing or terms, while the marketing stakeholders are often looking to get the right-sized team with the right qualifications. This lack of alignment on the client side can contribute (at least partially and often accidentally), to a tough MSA/SOW negotiation with the new darling agency.

Ideally speaking, there would be a better role sort during negotiations without the masking of who actually is in charge. Here are a few things that can really help negotiations and further grow trust during this tense moment in time.

1. **Be clear about who makes the call** — Too often the case is that the procurement leader is positioned as the person making the final call when the truth is the client is doing so. Games help nobody. Ultimately, it's the best use of everyone's time to just explain the role of each party in the negotiation, whether it's operations, procurement, or client/marketing. Each party indeed has

a critical role, but ideally, those roles are shared with the negotiating partner. This is not about power, but rather understanding who makes what call and why.

2. Team negotiations help both parties — Ideally, big moments in the negotiation process would have a triangle of parties involved including the client sponsor, the procurement team (if this exists), and finally the agency. Long after owners and lawyers move on, the work is left to the client and agency leads to get the work done, so best to ensure their inclusion. In fact, it is a great test of the future partnership to watch how parties negotiate during this first trial.

3. Agency operations should always have a say beyond just sales — Often, the operations group is consulted either too late in the game or not at all. This happens because frankly, it's easier to push a deal across the table without diving into the details. This hurts both the agency *and* the client. The complexity of the relationship has to make it to the operations groups on both the client and agency sides so that the people close to the trenches can debate the details. If you spare the details early, you will hurt longer later. So, building on the previous point, include the operations people wherever possible. They know how and where the gears grind and can include a dose of reality. Sometimes we don't want to hear those practical voices, but in reality, it's in our collective best interests to hear those details and make sure they are addressed in the negotiation.

While these three points give you a good list of things to contemplate in terms of people and process, I will provide a few pro tips for key negotiation points to really lift the cover on what is going on for both sides, in the hopes of helping the industry get to more mutual wins. Let's review a few critical challenges that are created and how to deal with each set of challenges.

1. No limitation or cap on liability — One of the most common areas of debate in an MSA is the question of how to cap risk. If left to a client, they might shift unlimited risk to the agency. The agency wishes to reduce the risk. When all of the risks are shifted to the agency, you don't get their best work because the wildest ideas also possess the most risk. What in turn happens is that agencies shy away from user-generated content, innovative yet riskier creators, and envelope-pushing ideas.

Instead try — Allow the agency to cap their liability at the ceiling of their insurance policy. This allows them to shoulder plenty of risk which will keep them in check, but it will also allow them to work, fight, and take risks on behalf of the client and bring forth great ideas. Or maybe, consider allowing the agency to cap their risk at the ceiling of their fee; why would they want to risk more than they are going to earn?

Instead try — Carve out the specific risks you are most worried about. If you as a client are most worried about an agency misusing your marks for example, make the punishment focused on an infraction in this specific area, versus broadly pushing all risk to the agency.

2. Unrealistic payment terms that are 90+ — There has been a lot written about some larger multinational companies forcing Net 120+ day terms on agencies. This is just not acceptable, effectively asking an agency to become a bank for the client. It creates horrible misalignment as agencies often have to pay vendors in Net 30- to Net 60-day terms. I have watched agencies go out of business by getting squeezed in that middle.

Instead try — Thirty- to sixty-day terms, depending on size and scope. You want your agency to be economically healthy. Agencies that are not healthy end up taking shortcuts on the work. This helps no one.

3. Avoid focusing too much on hours and don't overpack the SOW with details — While the first two are the hot items of the MSA, I would also address two big elements of the SOW negotiation, which are even more important than the MSA.

The scourge of hours — Attempt to avoid auditing and focusing on hours. The agency I co-founded, Acadia, with my partner Sean Belnick, avoids tracking hours wherever we are able. Instead, we believe that we have a job to do, and a fee a client has agreed to pay for that work. Sometimes, that will mean more hours, and other times less. We are a bit unique (proudly so) in this regard. If you decide you must track hours, that is okay, but my recommendation is to not make that the focal point. The reason for this is that agencies will play the hours game if this is the main element that is tracked. Focus on deliverables, tasks, commitments, and milestones—not on hours. Focus on outputs, quality, and team. Focus on what matters in the negotiation and then the agency will measure what matters. When hours are the focus, very sadly, agencies load hours into the systems.

Be careful to not put every single contemplated task in an SOW — Sometimes an SOW is overpacked with details. When there are too many details, there is no room for interpretation. In these cases of over-thoroughness, the account leader on the agency side tends to spend more time focusing on the checklist of items to accomplish instead of potential needle-moving items.

Very simply, if you remember any one single thing from this chapter, it should be this: negotiations must always include the two parties who are going to spend the most time together in the future and that these parties understand what the work needs to look like. Guard against the temptation for an MSA/SOW negotiation to be one of opposing positions, but instead look at it as collaboratively achieving a deal fostering a team and work product that pleases everyone. And, in the end, the only win will be one in which both parties truly believe they left a bit on the table. Because if the client truly "wins" the negotiation, they don't really win in the end. If the agency "wins" the negotiation, there will be resentment later, as they did not really win, either.

Compromise is the only real win.

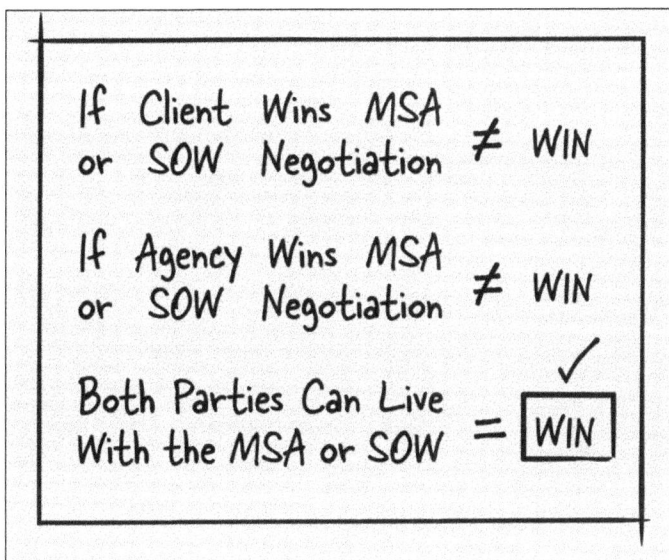

If Client Wins MSA
or SOW Negotiation   ≠ WIN

If Agency Wins MSA
or SOW Negotiation   ≠ WIN

Both Parties Can Live
With the MSA or SOW   = WIN ✓

CHAPTER 5

How to Inspire Great Work

There are many ways to inspire great work and output from your agency partner. To some degree, the right strategy is the one that fits you, the client. You can't be someone else. My goal in this chapter is to put forth a few things I have seen that have gone a long way to inspire an agency to bring its A-game. The menu below is varied in the hope that maybe a few items can feel right for you to adapt yourself.

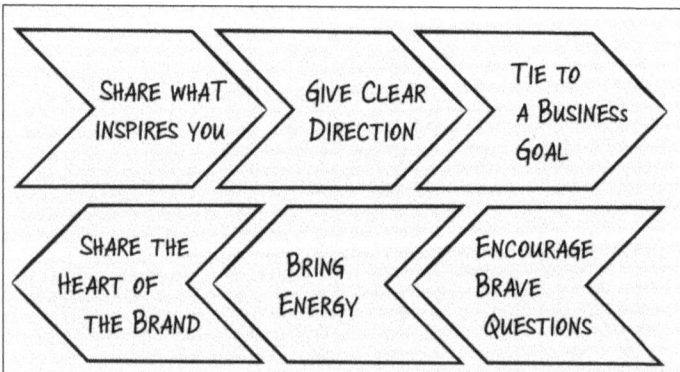

1. Share what inspires you — One of the most impressive moments for me was on a pre-kickoff call for Burger King with Fernando Machado briefing us. For those of you who don't know of Fernando, he is a fairly well-known CMO, recognized for inspiring breakthrough work. I first got to meet Fernando on what turned out to be a pre-brief. My assumption going in was that it would be more of a classic kickoff where Fernando would share a bit about Burger King, share a bit about the campaign challenge, and then share a few particulars. However, in all the best ways, it turned out to be something else.

He took the full hour to share advertising that inspired him throughout the history of Burger King. He went back to the 80s and then the 90s. He beamed with enthusiasm for the craft of creative. Not only was I energized, but the creatives around me felt like they had died and gone to Heaven. If you want to inspire great work from your agency, why not show them what inspires you?

I share the above story because it is so simple. It feels at times that clients are pressured to be robotic and perfect. Agencies respond to humanity, vulnerability, and passion. Share pictures, share stories, and tell us about your family and passions. Share work, hopes, and ambitions, and what "great" is to you.

2. Give very clear direction — Diahann Young, now a marketing leader at PulteGroup, was my boss while she was leading the Fanta brand at Coca-Cola. Diahann was incredible at repeating, reminding, and simplifying. Diahann was clear that Fanta stood for a playful escape into a land of fruit-flavored fun. She would repeat this to begin every call. She would repeat it when a brief went off the rails. She would repeat it when giving any creative feedback. She would repeat this when a creative or media choice was made that was too serious or too adult-oriented. She believed that this repetition of the core positioning would make it such that all agency partners would stay on track, stay inspired, and stay clear-headed.

You might ask, "Is clarity really an ingredient of inspiration?" The short answer is yes. Nothing is more inspiring than clarity.

3. Tie your marketing challenge to a greater business goal — One of the most impressive moments I ever recall in a briefing was one that was hosted by the former president of Chili's, Steve Provost (as of this writing, he is the inspiring leader over at Maggiano's). Steve got us all in a room and helped us to understand the situation. He, along with a very talented team, decided to invest more money in the menu, the physical space, and the operations of the restaurant. He reminded us, "It does not matter how great the advertising is, if the menu, the space, and the service are not all Grade A. So, what I need from you all is to make our media plan even more effective than it used to be, but with $X million less in media."

As such, what he needed from our media team was to deliver greater impact via media but for $X million fewer dollars even in the face of media inflation. Tying our media brief back to the business need, and knowing our work could impact thousands of jobs, gave it greater meaning. Steve found a way to make sure our work felt like it mattered.

4. Share the heartbeat of your brand — Justin Hackney, SVP of Media/Marketing of Bark, has been an inspiring client of ours at Acadia. Justin, though, is the first guy to tell you he does not inspire via grandiose speeches. Instead, Justin inspires via mission and focus. Bark is a company on a mission to help protect the world from adverse aspects of digital marketing.

When it was time for our onboarding, Justin took the right amount of time to make our team feel part of the mission. Even though we were "just doing SEO," we felt that every number-one ranking we could secure for Justin and Bark would be more families protected from cyber-bullying and body-shaming (part of the mission for Bark).

5. Bring energy to the weekly call — I know this seems basic, but you might not know how much this matters. Every week for most engagements is a weekly client-agency call. Typically, the agency prepares for this call by ensuring there is a good agenda, a crisp item to present, and a list of things that need to get done or things that need to get out of a log jam. This weekly call is a big deal to a great agency team. They organize, prepare, and rehearse. What happens, though, over time is that both parties show up to these common status calls without enough energy. In short, both parties start to wear sweatpants. Energy is the heartbeat of our industry.

Ellie Doty, former CMO of Chili's and Burger King, was incredible at bringing energy to every call and meeting she ever attended. She leaned in, asked questions, and would take an active interest in the entire team down to the mid-level account manager. She got to know the team and she made it a point to appreciate how things got made and created.

This intense enthusiasm and humanity created an atmosphere where the team would fight for her. This is the lesson for you to take away as a great client. Every agency essentially has two types of clients—clients whom the best talent wants to work for, and clients whom the A+ talent wants to run from. With Ellie, the word got out and the A+ talent always wanted to run to work and fight for her.

6. Encourage the agency to ask big questions — The former CEO of InterContinental Hotels Group, Andrew Cosslett, said in an interview with Adam Bryant, "In every business I've worked in, there's been a lot of cost and value locked up in things that are deemed to be 'the way we do things around here.' I just keep asking people 'why do you do that?'"

The point here is that a great client creates huge value for them, their business, and the agency team when they ask bigger questions. There is power in encouraging an agency to ask, "why must we do X this way?" or "what if there were no prior year to model?" and "what would we do differently?"

With this in mind, the ability to ask great questions that might unlock value starts with the client modeling this behavior. One of our clients, Scott Hargrove, CMO of California Pizza Kitchen, is great at this. Because he has such humility, he is always brave enough to ask hard and thoughtful questions. In a world in which he had a limited budget, he encouraged us to question everything, even things that are understood as conventional wisdom. This led the team to question the amount of funding for "brand search" (something that is literally sacred in many circles), when the goal was to drive new traffic into the restaurants.

7. Gratitude is a superpower for the super client — The current CMO of 7-Eleven, Marissa Jarratt, puts on a masterclass on the power of gratitude at every turn. I recall a time when the agency had a real fire in our offices and so the office was a mess, people had been dislocated from their cubes, and everyone was on edge. Marissa and her team happened to visit our offices right around that time, because of a scheduled launch.

She settled into her chair, and she opened the meeting by thanking the team for being all-in on 7-Eleven while dealing with this fire. She went around the room ensuring that everyone was acknowledged, from the most senior person to the most junior person. For Marissa, this was not a sporadic thing—it was an all-the-time thing. She would always make a point of showing appreciation to the junior planner who never gets thanked or the social media manager. Her demonstration of gratitude was not just verbal, but also through body language. She always leans in, asks thoughtful questions, and tries to understand where you are coming from. This all leads to an agency feeling motivated and wanting to work harder.

All too often, clients think they are buying the "agency brand" when they are mostly buying the "agency team" they are paired with. When the client inspires their agency team with enthusiasm and clarity, as well as making them feel part of the team, they get highly focused and ambitious collaborators. If you just mail it in, you get that same vibe and level of productivity back in return. Being the best possible client in this regard is not just an ideal, but an economic imperative.

CHAPTER 6

What to Keep In-House and When to Use an Agency

What should I keep in-house (i.e.—do with teams inside your company's four walls) versus when do I use an agency? This may be one of the most persistent struggles I hear about. In the zeitgeist of advertising, there is a lot of back and forth around this issue, particularly while weathering different economic cycles. This is a hugely consequential decision and therefore it would be ideal to apply some sort of lens that can hopefully help you make some sense of all the noise around this topic.

Yes, I've worked at agencies all my career, but have also had a few turns as a client and board member, so my hope is that this makes me qualified to share with you why you need to at least grapple with this very difficult decision. I want to provide four key areas to guide your decision: *your core*, *economics*, *resource scarcity*, and *leverage*. Let's look at each one.

Is it at your core?

Not every client is suited to in-house media, creative, analytics, or whatever service you might be talking about. A key question to ask yourself is, "How core is this service to the essence of my company, its mission, and its talent base?"

Let's look at an example. For about eight years, I was on a team that proudly served as Capital One's digital media and analytics agency. Capital One was an incredible client and our team did some great work for them over those eight years. Toward the end of year seven, they were incredibly honest (shout-out to them and their great culture of integrity) and indicated they needed to bring most of their digital media and analytics in-house. Their reason for the change was a great lesson I have held on to for years. They shared, "Capital One is as much a data company as it is a credit card company, so we naturally have to be close to our customer acquisition data."

They had more data engineers at Capital One than most of the modern digital advertising agency complex combined, so of course that made sense. Capital One had the ability, the engineering capability, the will, and the business mandate to get closer to their data. To be clear, they did not bring "everything" in-house. They continued to delegate their TV media-buying to an agency and continued to use a great roster of other agencies for social media and campaign creative because those pursuits were not core to their culture in the same way that digital media and analytics were.

It is important for your brand to really think hard about whether you have the internal DNA and team to be the best at media, digital, analytics, creative, social, SEO, and associated services. Is this core to your business and your strengths? If the answer is no, it's a good initial signal to recognize it would be productive to partner (at least partially) for the biggest possible return.

Economics

The weakest argument for keeping work in-house is typically the economic argument. Too often, a hastily created cost savings case is fashioned essentially comparing a banana and a lamp in the cost exercise. In other words, the analysis too often does not compare the right things, which in turn leads to a false conclusion as to whether there are real savings. Don't get me wrong, there might well be, but it's important to be sure you have looked at the right areas and compared the right things. Here are things that need to be included when a client is trying to examine if the costs are lower than the fees they are paying the agency.

1. **Benefits, healthcare, and overhead** — When you figure out your true cost of staff in-house, you have to take care to multiply this by at least a 1.5 salary

multiplier to account for benefits, healthcare, et al. Too often this step is forgotten. The 1.5-multiplier is likely light (it can often be far higher), but it's a place to start. Simply put, you are paying for far more than just salaries when employees are on your client-side payroll, and your business case must account for this to be accurate.

2. Attrition and hiring — When you have a three-person team running search, creative, or social (as examples) for you in-house, and one person leaves, it might take you three months in this current hiring climate to replace them. Those are three months of lost productivity with no bench to pick from. Furthermore, the burden on the other two who remain creates a situation where they are more likely to leave as well. In this reality, you have to model that opportunity cost (lost productivity) when there is eventual productivity loss due to being short-staffed.

It is key to ask yourself, "Would a search marketing or social media all-star want to leave their current job to come and work for me at this XYZ company?" You know the real answer here deep down. If you are the new hot retailer, the answer might be a resounding yes. If you are an old-fashioned steel company, that pays towards the lower end, perhaps the answer is no. Either way, do some reflection to figure out which type you are.

3. Tech savings — There are many technology providers that an agency uses on your behalf. It might include things like DSP, DMP, Data Lake, Clean Room, ad-serving fees, API connections, competitive research tools, creative testing tools, and the like. Typically, an agency will have a superior rate due to the volume they do with those providers which could be 10 to 30% cheaper than when a client goes direct.

The larger agencies have favored rates with the likes of Google, The Trade Desk, Salesforce, and so on. They also have favored rates with certain publishers, partners, and providers. They have those rates because of the billions in aggregate spending they bring forth to those mega-platforms. While you still might have a significant budget at say $20 million, if you are now having to pay 2% more for an access fee to a demand side platform (DSP), that could potentially be another big slog of tech fees you are having to pay out (depending, of course, on the amount that goes through the chosen platform) that would completely negate any sort of savings argument of going in-house. Again, there are no right answers but you must do the math that's in the weeds, not just the surface calculations.

4. Invisible perspective/expertise tax — You get more than just your agency team when you get an agency. Let's pretend you are a client hiring an agency in organic social. Sure, you have a team of five FTEs who are there to do a job around social creative. However, when you have a question around GA4, Tagging, or some other web analytics question, you can tap into that overall agency expertise that sort of comes with the premium to do something outside. To some degree, your agency is your all-around "phone a friend" partner.

5.   The cost of not being on the bleeding edge — Beta's, Alpha's, Tests, the newest tech, and the newest methods typically start with a great agency. If you are a conservative CPG entity, it's entirely possible/probable that your team is already busy and does not have time to figure out what is on the cutting edge of consumer desires. It's just difficult. Agencies do this by a function of how they work. They work across so many industries and challenges, that innovation is just a natural by-product. Be careful not to underestimate this loss.

Resource scarcity

It is very difficult for an auto parts online warehouse in Kansas City to hire a twenty-person data science team. Yes, I understand that in theory, the remote world helps change that dynamic, but bear with me on the argument. Let's talk about why. A great data scientist (insert whatever function you want here) is scarce. They can work at Google, Tesla, or NASA. They can work at the hottest EV car company or the coolest start-up. They can work at an agency that is doing groundbreaking work. Yes, they can work in Kansas City for an auto parts company as well.

I'm just suggesting that it's harder than you think,

even with the recent proliferation of remote work. The best guidance I can provide here is to spend time with HR and a professional recruiter assessing the odds of building out the team, at the salaries you assume and on the timeline you estimate, and factor this into your decision.

As of this writing, there is an average "time to fill" of ninety days for top digital talent. When the brand you are hiring for or the salary you have to offer is not top-notch, this lag can be even longer. This lag is enough to truly destabilize your plans if not planned for and managed.

Leverage

At times, using an agency is about leverage. There are certain activities where leverage is required and even ideal. A great example of this is TV buying, especially TV buys in what is referred to as the "upfronts." If you are a larger TV advertising spender, and you want to ensure your ads end up in primetime on a very popular TV show, chances are you will have an advantage in buying within the context of a larger holding company.

There can be leverage in creativity as well. If you have a quick summer campaign or re-brand that is about to happen, or maybe you are releasing a new product or movie, these "once a year" moments have to be perfect. When you are short on time, and the stakes are high, there is often a need to get more great minds in a room.

At an agency, you can quickly source those vast

perspectives in a way that may not be possible within your own four walls. Again, there is no right answer, other than to ensure you look back at your average year and ask yourselves, when do I need the leverage my agency can bring forward for me?

Not all or nothing

Above all else consider not framing the choice as a binary one. It is not "in-house versus agency." The choice here can be nuanced by service and industry.

You have a big choice to make when thinking of in-housing versus working with agencies. Hopefully, this framework was useful. Think in terms of *economics, leverage, scarcity,* and finally *core.* Consider using the following worksheet.

	WITH AGENCY	IN-HOUSE
ECONOMICS		
LEVERAGE		
RESOURCE SCARCITY		
CORE		

CHAPTER 7

Therapy is Cheaper than Divorce

At some point, you are going to want to fire your agency. This might even be a feeling that comes to you a few times a year. Heck, it might even happen three weeks in, and you have that "what the heck have I done?" sort of feeling. You might even feel that as you read this paragraph. That is a natural emotion, but likely not a healthy or productive one.

If you were not pleased with an internal employee, you would certainly invest in them and work to coach them up. Why should it be any different with so much invested and at stake? My main message is to challenge that feeling, spend time investing in the marriage, and consider therapy over divorce. I find that when times are stressful, the healthiest thing you can do is to ask yourself some questions. In short, spend a few minutes trying to figure out your role in the problem. Surely, it's not as one-sided as it might seem, so here are a few key questions to ask:

1. **Is it possible the problem is partially owned by you?** — I am not writing this merely as a biased agency leader, but rather as someone who has been a client in two very different circumstances. Both working at Coca-Cola and then again for a smaller lawn-and-garden company called Dynamite Plant Food, I was simply not a great client to my agencies. My briefs were rushed and lazy. My instructions were vague with speedy turnarounds. My feedback was clipped. So, all I am suggesting is that you reflect a little bit.

2. **Is it possible the problem is one or two team members and not the agency?** — An agency team could be as small as two people or as big as fifty. It's important to understand if your disappointment is a personnel issue or a fundamental agency mismatch.

In most team situations with an agency, you get 80% of your information via two to three key people. If those folks don't match your style or the way you like to receive information, the feeling you have towards the agency will be dramatically effected. Take stock. Is the work overall good? Are the results overall good? Are you simply irritated by the account person or the lead creative director? Could it be that the lead analyst talks down to you and is a bit disorganized? Own it, try and improve it, but most of all, speak up and ask for a change in personnel versus throwing out the baby with the bathwater.

3. **Are the results the problem, and not the**

agency? — This will be a very controversial thing to write, but it's important to understand that an agency can't turn around results by itself. I was once working with a very large retail department store brand, whose sales had been eroding due to style changes, direct-to-consumer (DTC) buying habits, and 20% reductions to marketing spend, yet the client kept wanting to see us post 10%+ numbers. This was as likely as my dog mastering how to play the trumpet.

In these situations, the key is for the client to reflect and truly ask if their results and expectations are reasonable. When an agency is forced to chase an impossible goal, a very quick death spiral starts.

What you often see is that the client is angry you are not reaching the 10% goal, the team believes they are in a no-win situation, and the best team members ask to be removed from the account or quit. Then the remaining team members are put in a defensive position, believing it's not worth their time to bring new ideas to the fold.

4. Have you sent flowers lately or are you just wearing sweatpants to the relationship? — When an agency receives food for the team, a thank you note, or better yet free product, the team goes wild. It's so unexpected. It feels like a total shot of adrenaline. Emails and Slack messages fly around with pride realizing the client took a minute to acknowledge all the hard and often unseen work.

Have you told them lately that you love them? Agency people are poet-warriors. They are hard-charging and optimistic in one regard, but sensitive souls waking up to please you in another regard. For $50 in goods and postage, you can create huge motivation. Note, this does not need to be a true care package (i.e. what you send does not matter compared to the gesture given how rare it is). This might be a hand-written note or some sort of more casual thank you. The point still is the same—a little thanks and surprise go a long way because it is so rare.

Taking a step back, the goal here is to take the emotion out of the "do I want to fire my agency?" gut feeling. The intention is to make this slightly more analytical. Perhaps you want to consider doing a little five-point self-reflection exercise. This very easy, and very free, self-questionnaire that follows might save you a lot of time, money, and aggravation.

Do you dislike most elements of the agency, or do you truly just dislike one to two members of the team?

- ☐ I dislike most elements of the agency.
- ☐ I dislike one to two members of the team.
- ☐ Neither/Not sure

	Yes	No
Have you given formal, written, or verbal feedback to the agency in the last three months?	☐	☐
Have your briefs, budgets, and goals been clear and correct?	☐	☐
Is the person managing the agency relationship someone known for getting the most out of large teams?	☐	☐

What is your best alternative and are you sure it is better? What is your reasoning?

_____
_____
_____
_____
_____

After you have done this self-reflection exercise, and you still feel the relationship is in trouble, there are a few things to try from there:

1. Ask for a reset meeting — Instead of wishing that the agency improves on its own, write up your ideas into a one-pager, and ask the agency for a "reset" to include the CEO of the agency (so it gets proper attention), the agency team lead, and the top two subject matter experts. Be clear on four things:

A. What is not working?
B. What alternatives do you wish for?
C. On what dates would you like to see the changes?

D. What scorecard will be used to evaluate changes?

Make sure this meeting gets proper time on a calendar and, if an in-person meeting is possible, go for that option.

2. Work with a third party — There are many companies that help clients and agencies see through hard times. Very often both parties need a third party to allow them to talk freely about what is hampering great work, and how to dislodge that feeling. A great third-party peace broker will take the time to survey multiple parties on both sides of the fence, look to build understanding and empathy around gaps, take the emotion out of the process, and allow for more critical reviewing. This is often difficult for clients to do because of friendships that develop over time.

Then, and only then, is the time to issue a ninety-day notice and start the process of moving on. People stay with lawyers, accountants, dentists, doctors, painters, and plumbers for decades at a time. Why is this one industry rife with breakups after less than two years? There is no one single answer, but more patience and openness from both parties will help.

CHAPTER 8

How to Provide Effective Feedback to Your Agency

One of the most important duties of a great client is to give feedback. This could come in the form of giving feedback on work, a strategy plan, a campaign wrap report, or simply on a social media post. Each one of those moments of feedback is a chance for you to motivate and get the best work from your team. There is an art and a science to it, and the hope is that the following strategies may allow you to get the most out of each feedback session with your agency teams.

1. Focus on feelings, not blame and personal attacks — Countless books suggest you tell your partner or spouse how a situation makes you feel rather than focusing on his or her behavior. Saying "I feel *anxious* when you're late coming home and haven't called" is more likely to result in a productive discussion than "You're always late! What were you doing? Why do you do this to me?" Accusations more often bring defensiveness and the escalation of *anger* rather than rational discussions.

This is just as true in client-agency relationships as it is in a marriage. You very much can share a feeling that "the creative presentation was missing a bit of the usual energy" but it's less productive to say that "Jason is a boring presenter."

2. Avoid escalation right away — Too often, a client goes above the day-to-day team members and calls their executive sponsor on the agency side right away. While this might feel like the most efficient thing to do, it erodes trust with the day-to-day team. If you have feedback on the analysis, share it with the analyst first. If you have feedback on the copy, try and share it with the copywriter. If you have feedback on the media plan, the media supervisor who did the actual negotiation is just a call or a Slack message away.

This is not to say you don't have the right to escalate. However, there is immense power in direct, initial feedback to the person who did the work, and thus knows the most about it.

3. Ground feedback in facts — The quickest way to frustrate your agency partner is to start a sentence by saying, "I think" or "I believe," because this suggests the evaluation comes only from your gut, rather than factual information. As a client, you have more tools at your fingertips beyond belief. You can reference data, history, competition, brand, goals, and finally the agreed-upon brief.

Try this phrasing below instead:

Jason, your work was great. The issue is that the margin gained on children's dress clothes is inferior to that of designer women's clothing. Your work was thoughtful, but we are going in a new direction. We are going to put the children's concept to the side and focus 100% of the team's energy on the designer looks with two new versions requested within ten business days.

4. It's always about the brand — When giving feedback, your ironclad strongest backstop is what the brand stands for, not what you stand for. If you are running Red Bull, and your brand stands for energy, then it is fully within your right to tell the agency "I appreciate your efforts, but the ad just does not have enough signals of Energy, and as we all know, that is the core proposition of the brand."

As a client, nobody knows more about the brand than you do. When I was working as an associate brand manager of Fanta, at one point our agency misunderstood the brief a bit and took the brand in too much of a serious direction. I coached the agency to remember that Fanta stood for fruity, fun, and playful experiences. This allowed me to focus the feedback on the brand, rather than appearing that the feedback came from my gut.

If you find yourself saying "that is too yellow," "that copy has no hook," or "those keywords will never work" just count to ten and rephrase in a way that brings the feedback back to the brand.

5. Focus on the brief and the challenge, not the person — Teams often take a lot of time to settle on a brief. The brief in the marketing services business is meant to be both a compact and a North Star. It is meant to be a short summary of what you are trying to achieve with a given campaign or initiative, and then what has been agreed upon between the client and agency. However, we often see a situation where all the parties spend days on landing a brief, but then fail to use it as a true North Star. When this happens, situations devolve into commentary about individuals on the team.

When work goes off the rails, re-share the physical brief/email/stimuli and just circle the relevant part. Take the personal out of it and focus the debate on the brief, and away from the person. You might say something like, "In the brief, we agreed to 'value' as a key construct, yet 80% of this ad copy does not mention price. Can you help me understand how you see your work landing the 'value' element of the brief?"

If you can focus on keeping feedback fact-based and non-emotional, you can be better at persuading, and keep the temperature lower. Practice the five-step process in the illustration that follows to give better feedback.

HOW TO GIVE GREAT FEEDBACK TO YOUR AGENCY / PARTNER

No blame	Avoid escalation	Never say "I believe"
①	②	③

Always about the brand	Focus on the brief
④	⑤

CHAPTER 9

One Goal is Better than Three

Clients deserve to have a number of nuanced goals. The question, though, is not what a client deserves, but rather what is in their best interest and will net them the best ROI.

I worked with a sports retail client for a period of time. They wanted volume, a very high return on ad spend (ROAS), high margin, and also periodically wanted to put money into the mid-funnel (i.e., create some consideration and awareness as well) in support of new product-line announcements. These four goals are very reasonable when examined individually, however, they were constantly moving and therefore at odds with each other.

High ROAS for example is possible when you are focused on selling core products in tried-and-true channels (Search as an example). However, let's just say that Search is yielding a 5:1 ROAS. The minute you try and double your investment into that channel, the

ROAS will drop on average, and often the last 10% of that budget will have a poor ROAS. Enter: a tug-of-war with volume (another stated goal). Now your previously successful media team feels it's failing in your eyes.

Further, as we tried more mid-funnel activities like influencer marketing and online video in support of those new product lines, the ROAS was no longer as high. The CFO sees this and says, "Let's get that video/ IM investment out and put it back into what's working!"

Ah. "What's working" is arguably the most interesting comment here. With media investment, nothing ever "works" or "doesn't work." Rather it's relative to what objective was set—if it were ever correct in the first place. More on that soon.

It's very hard to have *good, fast,* and *cheap* at the same time. Something has to give. It's a bit hard to have volume, ROAS, and also brand-building happening all at the same moment. Again, to be super clear, I am not mocking this client at all. It is very human to want all of these goals, and in an abstract way, the combination of them all would be great for business. The issue simply comes down to the fact that three to four goals are often counterproductive to how the real work gets done.

The previous story is one that I have seen play out one hundred times. This happens with creative where someone wants the video creative to "drive passion for the brand" but also "drive immediate sales." Can those two things exist at once? Sure, if you find lightning in a bottle, but generally speaking, once you start to have too many conflicting goals, you end up with beige khaki pants, which nobody ever goes to a store wanting to buy—and you end up just settling, and settling never makes anyone happy. I don't think this is an agency problem or a client problem, I think it's an issue of briefing, measurement rigor, and to some degree, patience.

In an ideal world, the way a client could brief an agency regarding their goals would be something like this:

1. Name the objective for your overall marketing program and communications plan — This might be where you state the goal of the overall investment is to position your brand as the go-to apparel solution for rugged, woodsy dads on the go. This helps set the tone that the "reason we are doing marketing in the first place is to build this brand to be beloved by rugged, outdoorsy dads."

2. Name the objectives and corresponding measurement KPIs for each slug of spend in the communications plan — What do you expect Search to do and how should it perform, versus the role of Video? Yes, the agency will of course have a POV, but it's worthwhile to share your own POV so expectations are set or at least debate can be had.

This way, when it's getting hot in the kitchen, and your CFO is asking you why ROAS is low for Video, you don't cancel it but rather are able to explain it. This is so critical because if you don't agree upfront about which KPI will assess each tactic, then it becomes very easy to have selective memory take over as the campaign starts to spend, panic ensues, and you start wanting to cut everything with a poor ROAS, even though you know you had certain tactics to help build a brand. Short story long, agree early on which medium does what, and how it will be measured, and stick to that plan.

Beyond the above, the service I want to provide here for clients reading this book is to really appreciate the downhill ramifications around goal setting. How you set goals and stick to them puts your partners in the best possible place to help you and your shareholders succeed.

When you share conflicting or confusing goals with your agency, they have to plan, re-plan, and re-brief their own partners. This creates a great deal of makework that essentially dilutes the power of your team to create results for you. Your agency's hours are really your hours, and so anything you can do to not waste those hours is critical.

If I were to suggest just one book on the topic of goal-setting, it would be John Doerr's *Measure What Matters*. Doerr lays out how to really harness the power of Objectives and Key Results far beyond how I mentioned them above. There are two key things to keep in mind that you might use when briefing an agency on your goals.

1. An objective is simply what is to be achieved — It should be concrete, significant, and motivating. It is clarifying. Things like "Win Q4 by showing the world we are the most innovative brand in shaving" or "Demonstrate to all pet owners that brand X provides excellent nutrition while having the smallest environmental footprint."

2. A Key Result is specific, time-bound, measurable, and verifiable — You cannot have a key result without a number. This is something like "raise awareness of your core target by 10% within the next six months." This is specific, time-bound, and very much measurable.

The interesting thing here is that most clients have terrific objectives for their own companies, yet less than stellar goals and objectives for their agency partners. Trust me, if you take the time to deliver to your agency clear, measurable, and stable goals, they will have higher probability odds of succeeding.

CHAPTER 10

Seek Out a Great Executive Sponsor Relationship

Every client deserves to know that the leadership of their partner agency cares about them. There are many ways for that care, passion, and focus to be shown, but a favorite of mine is executive sponsorship.

Before going any further, what is an executive sponsor? There is not any one singular definition but, for the purposes of this book, it is a senior and experienced executive on the agency side who is empowered to help make changes, adjustments, and improvements to the team. They have the skillset to actively listen and anticipate problems and opportunities at a high level in partnership with a senior client. About once a quarter there are very large and important decisions that might need to be made. This list could include things like the following:

1. Approval of staffing or fee changes
2. Review of a radical change in strategy
3. Partnership on a deck that is going up the ladder

to the CEO and board of directors

4. Approval of a controversial saying/image/idea that might have legal complexity

5. Approval for a big (but strategic) increase in the production budget to get the right director/actor that just became available

6. Major changes to a staffing model

7. A significant change to KPIs or goals

These types of decisions, and many others like them, benefit from having an executive-sponsor relationship. These types of decisions require seniority and the ability to rise above some of the day-to-day. So, what might a great executive sponsor look like for you?

A great executive sponsor fights for you

Your agency relationship is going to have down moments. There are going to be moments when you don't like the work. Moments where the ROI is down. Moments where creative is launched incorrectly. Moments where key staff leaves the team or some rotation is needed. Moments where the board of directors is leaning on you, and you need to in turn get more out of the agency. Moments of critical conversation. Moments where a change of scope is needed. These moments are all but guaranteed. In these moments, the agency-client dynamic needs strong involvement from an executive sponsor.

Be in touch with a client's ambitions— are they leaping or stepping?

It's been my experience that most moments where clients are making an ask can be defined as either a "leaper" moment or a "stepper" moment. My friend Sarah Hofstetter, the president of Profitero, coined this phrase and I have always remembered it.

A stepper is a client who favors grinding out risk-adjusted small wins that have high odds of success. This might mean safer creative and smaller-but-thoughtful media bets. A leaper is someone willing to swing for the fences creatively and take some shots knowing there will be some strikeouts.

The point here is not that one is better than the other, but rather you find someone senior at the agency who gets you and helps the team understand if you prefer leaping or stepping at that moment. A great executive sponsor will understand this.

What I would say to you, the client, is that you don't need to think of yourself as one or the other. You can be a leaper at the start of the year when budgets are fresh, and the calendar still has twelve months to experiment, and then be a stepper come September when Q4 is staring you in the face, and pressure from the CFO and the board is mounting. Make sure you do not hide who you are at that moment, and be really honest and clear with your agency.

A great executive sponsor thinks about changes before you even suggest them

Inevitably, and as mentioned already in this book, things will go wrong in your agency relationship. Results, for example, may not be what you had envisioned or even what was promised. It happens. What is not inevitable though, is how these tough moments are handled.

An executive sponsor who is in touch with your business will not only know when problems arise, but they will have the confidence and bravery to suggest changes. For example, envision a situation where your agency might have a remit as the steward of your social media. Let's say that for whatever reason, there is no engagement, sales, or follower growth. A very able executive sponsor will spot this early, and perhaps suggest shifting some fee from social to search engine optimization (SEO), event marketing, or whatever the case may be. The story and tactics are not important, but rather the message that a great executive sponsor (as shown in the following image) can see a problem early and create guilt-free solutions before it becomes too late. If your agency has no executive sponsor, it often means the agency is a bit too late to spot challenges.

Overall, any great agency will be more than willing to provide an executive sponsor. If yours currently does not, just ask for one. You will be happy you did.

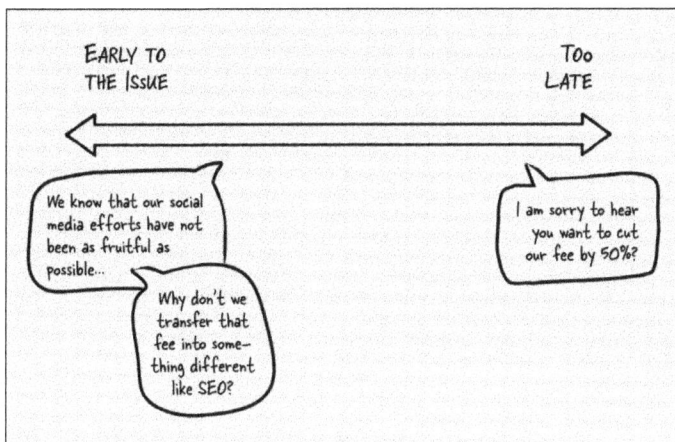

Section 2
TEN EMOTIONAL LESSONS

The second section of this book deals with the emotional understanding and nurturing needed for a special and productive relationship with your agency. Together we will navigate how to treat your agency as a true extension of your team, how to create alignment, and how to ensure you don't accidentally create a hunger-games-like environment between your agencies.

Then we'll focus on how to have better and more constructive debates with your partners and how to provide feedback that fuels the work and the soul. Ultimately, this section helps you better understand the personal current that pulses between the agency and the client. You begin to step back and realize you are hiring artists, poets, mathematicians, and sensitive souls who fundamentally wake up wanting to please you. Something indeed goes wrong from time to time, but for sure, they wake up wanting to please.

Some of these lessons allow you to shape the inherent underlying enthusiasm for clients that exist in every agency and become the master at making the most of it.

CHAPTER 11

Treat Your Agency as an Extension of Your Team

There are really only two types of accounts at an agency. There are accounts where A+ players want to run to and work on, and then there are accounts where people raise their hands by the minute to rotate off. It's that simple. You may have never thought about or heard this, but it's 100% true.

What it means is that you have the chance to be a great client, who creates an awesome environment where word gets out that it's incredible to work on your brand and for you. The difference between getting motivated "A" players who want to work for you versus "B" players who drudge to work each day is incredibly important.

I have seen clients do this well, and others do this poorly. I will share five specific examples where clients truly made their agency teams feel like extensions of their teams.

1. Make the entire team feel like they matter,

even the interns — Capital One was one of our largest clients at one of my former agencies. As a result, it had one of our largest teams. Top to toe, more than forty people touched the business. I was the managing director at the time and had the executive-sponsor relationship with the senior client.

During one of our 1:1 check-ins, he asked if he could come to Atlanta to visit with the team. Reflexively, I assumed he wanted to spend time with the most senior four to eight people, so I started to prattle on about that direction. He interrupted gently and said, "No Jared, I want a chance to spend time with all forty people."

Indeed, he started his visit with a two-hour talk introducing Capital One to everyone, from the business model to the core values. He made special efforts to speak directly to the most junior folks, making them feel very included. At night, he went out with us all to some random place that dressed you in a flight suit and allowed you to mimic the feeling of weightlessness. As we all left that night, just about every team member came up to me and shared that they felt such inclusion and were excited to be on the Capital One bus.

Hard to buy that with Zoom. Hard to buy that by just talking to the senior team members.

2. Don't tell the agency the answer, share the challenge — A great client shares a challenge and then works with the agency, with trust, as partners. Just like any relationship, you have to share information and be vulnerable in order to have a deeper relationship.

At Acadia, we have an incredible client in Red Roof Inn. All of our clients at Red Roof Inn are incredible and are ably led by Marina Macdonald, their CMO. She challenged us to find a way to make Red Roof Inn relevant in social. She challenged us to "find a lane" because all of the competitors had more money, brand awareness, and they were all chasing the same territory and consumers. We embraced the challenge and the trust, and in the end, were able to come up with Red Roofus (a mascot of sorts), leading to a pet-inspired Tik Tok strategy where we highlighted Red Roof Inn's pet-friendly policy and travelers' relationship with pets.

This led to Red Roof Inn being a major leader on Tik Tok and having a great run of increased bookings. Marina helped guide us by sharing a challenge, not by confining us to an answer. A challenge inspires, the answer stifles.

3. Not everything can be a fire — There is a fundamental difference between asking for a tracking tag to be updated on a site, requesting an update on a copy-test results readout, dealing with a change in copy in response to a legal/regulatory issue, and asking for a campaign presentation to be moved up by two weeks. Some of the above are wants, others are needs, and some are mandates.

A great client can share context with their agency

partner and be candid via signaling. "Team, I know this is a short turnaround, but please understand this is a board mandate because there is a controversial legal issue at hand." The point of this phrasing is that it provides context.

4. Clients who love the agency team will get loved back two-fold — One of my favorite clients ever, Harsha, is so cool and unique that he really just needs to go by that one name. Harsha loved us and fought for us and in return, he had a team of warriors who fought for him every day.

Harsha was the first to suggest we needed to celebrate wins together and would often work with me on details for team celebrations. Harsha was always the last one at the bar when these moments happened. He would spend that time talking not just to the senior members of the team, but saying hi to every junior member of the team. Harsha would fight for us to get legal and regulatory approval when it seemed like a long shot or if we needed to be protected. When we had wins in the data, Harsha was there with an email to our team celebrating the W.

Be that person your agency wants to fight for.

5. Great clients ask agencies to stretch, in the best ways — The term stretch often gets abused and overused. It too often means that a client tries to stretch out the team and get them to do far more than the SOW or deal structure allows. This leads to burnout on the team, which helps nobody.

The good version of the word stretch is best explained in Scott Sonenshein's book *Stretch*. His definition of stretching is the notion that great teams and leaders can make the most out of imperfect and often less abundant ingredients. They do this because necessity, creativity, and innovation all come together when you have less versus more. So, the notion here is that great clients give an agency just enough to get to great, but not so much that they cave under the weight. Challenge your agency to get scrappy and creative. They will thank you for it.

When you hire an agency, it's not like you bought an assembly line or a plastic blow mold device. When you bring on an agency, what you have really bought is a group of creative and analytical souls who desperately want to feel part of your mission and vision. The push and advice here are to spend as much time as you can spare making the agency feel relevant, wanted, and cared for. I promise you will get a major return on that.

CHAPTER 12

Have the Budget You Say You Have

Whether you are dealing with media, creative, or technology, the downstream effect of giving your agency a fishing errand with the wrong budget is harmful to all involved. For the purposes of this story, I am going to speak to media, but this story is the same for creative, technology, analytics, or any service.

I was being briefed by a national retailer and was told they had $30 million to spend on a rollout of a new product line. We were pumped. The stakes were high and our team was excited. With $30 million, there was so much we could do. We first did our research based on the $30 million and certain ROI targets, devising a strategy based on those calculations. The plan called for a focus on Video because we had to show the story of all the new products. We realized the plan would need to be 60% Video, broken out into CTV, OLV, Cable, and Prime. The other 40% would go to digital to speak to certain buying occasions using Google, Instagram, Facebook, and Tik Tok. Beyond that, we had two major broadcast partnerships with on-air integrations and four critical influencer marketing concepts.

Sadly, we soon found out the client just wanted to see "our best ideas" and that the real budget was closer to $10 million. This movie has played out thousands of times in hundreds of agency conference rooms around the country. Why is this not a victimless crime? After all, isn't this a reasonable motivational tactic by the client?

Here are the issues.

1.   There are different strategies with $10 million versus $30 million — If you had 33% fewer funds you absolutely would be looking to shift goals and focus. You might, for example, realize that $10 million allows you only to focus on the top ten markets and associated cable (versus broadcast). This million might only allow you to focus on a few important publishers, rather than spread your bets around. $10 million is different than $20 million!

2. Wasted time from publishers and research teams — Agencies issue RFPs (requests for proposals) to publishers and when there are budgets in the $30 million range, it means there is bespoke and original ideation happening with unique creative ideas. These take huge energy and time to create, and when the publisher finds out the budgets are not real, they feel frustrated and don't want to go to the idea well next time for that client.

3. Different CPMs with $200,000 than $500,000
-—When you have $30 million, you might have big slugs of $500,000 going to different partners who might in turn be able to offer unique rates that might not be available at smaller commitments associated with the smaller overall investment.

While on this topic, please also avoid the "gasoline" strategy. It's not like the 87, 89, and 93 octane choices at your local Exxon. Don't be that client who feeds the agency the classic "three scenarios" of $10 million, $20 million, and $30 million, when you know what you really have is closer to $10 million. Being generous, accurate, and clear creates mutual trust.

If you zoom out, you are trying to create a positive feedback loop and create good habits. In Charles Duhigg's incredible book, *The Power of Habit*, he finds an incredibly easy way to describe how great habits are created and hard-wired. There is a "cue," then a "routine," and finally a "reward."

The illustration for this process of trust-building around budgeting might look something like the illustration that follows. The client provides the cue which is a strategy and a budget. The agency then formulates a plan and investment strategy. From there, publishers and media sources are brought in to come up with interesting media placements.

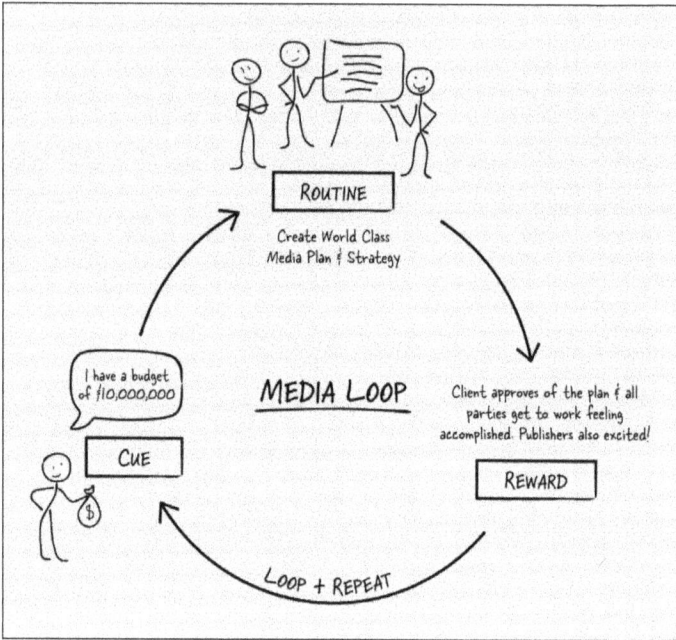

As a client, you are trying to create a virtuous cycle fed by trust of information, like you see in this visual.

Instead, if this briefing happens with a false budgetary level, the agency could spend up to 100 hours using its tools and people to create a strategy and investment plan that was rooted in poor guidance. That creates a huge loss of time and destruction of goodwill. From there, a multiplying effect is created due to hundreds of hours of publisher and partner time wasted.

Not only are those publishers upset and less likely to be as creative or accommodating next time, but they are out there at the bar talking about the brand in an unfavorable light. None of this is positive for the brand's reputation and it also de-motivates your team. So, when deciding to brief an agency or partner on a budget, get as close as you can to the real number and know you are doing the very right thing by giving as much transparency as you can provide. If you truly are not sure, just be generous and vulnerable in explaining why there is a potential variance. Your agency will love you for it.

CHAPTER 13

If You Want Better Answers, Ask Better Questions

Not too long ago, I had the privilege of sitting through a Zoom talk hosted by Navy captain David Marquet. The Captain is a retired United States Navy captain and bestselling author of both *Turn the Ship Around!* and *Leadership is Language.* He was the commander of the submarine USS Santa Fe and in his books covers the power of language and what it can signal as a leader. What jumped out at me, in particular, was that leaders too often can be accidentally coercive in the framing of their questions.

In reality, there are only two types of questions. One variety is a question that is self-affirming and closed. The other type is truly one of curiosity. Let's take a situation common in our world and look at the subtle, but massively important, distinction. Clients can at times inadvertently put agencies on the defensive via strained question patterns. You have the chance to be a unique client in which you ask insightful, open questions that allow you to get the best possible answers in return.

Let's pretend it's strategic planning time for the next year. The agency for whatever reason has decided that it would be a good idea to take $1 million in investment funds and make a $1 million bet on a high-profile influencer marketing partnership. That $1 million investment might be a great one, but there could be ten other places to place that investment bet. In reality, you are confused as to how they have made this seemingly ridiculous decision, and every part of you wants to bash it and ask sarcastic questions. I get it, you're human!

There is a long list of accidentally coercive questions that leaders ask, and that may have been asked in a situation such as the above where there is a feeling of doubt or skepticism.

Accidental yet coercive questions

- Is it (the influencer celebrity idea) safe?
- Are you sure this influencer will be popular in six months?
- Will it work?
- Will that prediction be true?
- Does that make sense?

Each one of those questions indicates in some way your displeasure and concern. Both emotions are fine and reasonable. However, if you want to discover why the agency had so much heart for this idea in the first place, you want to give them a shot to explain things, right? Each one of those questions above has a few easy but profound tweaks that can be made:

Improvements to achieve better explanations

- Change "Is it safe?" to *"How safe is it?"*
- Change "Will this influencer still be popular in six months?" to *"How confident are you that the influencer will be on trend in six months?"*
- Change "Will it work?" to *"What is the probability it will work?"*
- Change "Will that prediction be true?" to *"How confident are you in that prediction?"*
- Change "Does that make sense?" to *"How could I have made that clearer?"*

If you make this change away from coercive to curiosity-driven questioning, that draws out new information and you will notice a huge productivity increase in your team. The issue that may not seem obvious is that your question pattern has a lot more influence than you think. Agencies are anxious organisms despite all the fancy clothes and bravado. The best clients know how to pull out bravery from agencies versus shutting them down. Remember, if your team is afraid, you will get work, plans, and strategies that are timid. If you ask questions that stoke the imagination, you will get bravery in return.

CHAPTER 14

Your Agencies Might Hate Each Other Because of You, Not Them

Marketers often lament that their agencies fight with each other over territory. The irony here is that the vast majority of those issues happen not just because agencies behave badly, but more often because the client sponsor sets up a Shark Tank-like dynamic, without perhaps thinking through all the outcomes.

Let's examine the two most common manifestations of the issue and then talk about two very useful solutions:

Typical Problem 1: *The client gives vague swim lane assignments.*

I was once in a situation where a client, whom we will call Billy, created an agency ecosystem where our agency owned social, another agency owned paid social (media), and a third agency owned conceptual creative. In theory, this could work as all three of those tasks are different on paper. However, in reality, there is a high degree of overlap and codependency.

In this scenario, as the social agency, we were constantly taking our shot to move upstream and show the client we could do conceptual creative beyond organic social content. The conceptual creative agency kept trying to pitch social by-design ideas to elbow us out. And the media agency kept trying to throw both shops under the bus indicating their work was compromised by the creative's lack of clarity. Sigh. In the end, there was no trust among the agencies in the ecosystem.

Typical Problem 2: *The client creates too many jump balls without ground rules.*

A very popular modern thesis is to create an environment where "the best idea wins." Again, there is nothing wrong with this notion on paper. If I were a client, I might even consider elements of this ethos, as it's what's best for the consumer, shareholder, and outcome.

The issue here is that going after the jump ball takes far more investment than, well … just jumping for a ball. The agency must do insights work, strategy work, and creative specs work. What this means is that larger agencies with more people can chase more jump balls (advantage for them). Maybe the agency that has less financial discipline will chase more jump balls (but not usually the best one). Eventually, many agencies get tired of jumping when they don't understand the rules or enjoy the chaos.

What does a good relationship among different agencies look like?

With all this in mind, playing well in the sandbox together can be rewarded. Steve Provost, a client I deeply respect who at the time of this writing is leading Maggiano's, was incredible at creating good-spirited cooperation via clarity. Our agency had the media remit at that time, another agency (OKRP) had the creative, and a third agency had email and CRM. There was a clarity of communication, there was an expectation of data and insight sharing, and there was genuine cooperation. In addition, we all knew that trying to grab territory under the cover of darkness was not going to be rewarded. Steve actively encouraged collaboration and fairness.

There is nothing wrong with keeping your agency partners on their toes. Being an agency means always having to earn your seat at the table. The takeaway of this chapter is to pause and understand what it's like on the agency side when they are inadvertently pitted against each other. Agencies are most productive when they are motivated, yet have clear direction and objectives. The agency should be hungry to impress, while also clearly understanding their remit, standing, and role.

CHAPTER 15

The Investment You Make in Your Agency is Bigger than You Think

I had a client who always felt she had a small team. She always referred to her team as "lean and scrappy" in all the best ways. In many ways, she was right. A team of eight people managed a total marketing budget of tens of millions of dollars. Those eight people had to cover media, creative, CRM, loyalty, analytics, promotions, and more. They were very busy and never had enough time. In this regard, my client was very right.

It is interesting to note though that for this particular client, she also had an agency team of about ten FTEs (Full-Time Equivalents) on the team. Let's now pretend for a minute that the average cost of each FTE was about $270,000 (illustrative only) all in when you account for salary, benefits, and overhead. That accounts for $2.7 million in costs or 18,000 available hours that are all an extension of your team. I wanted this particular client to recognize that her team was not eight strong, but rather eighteen strong. While I suppose some would argue this to be semantics, it is not. It sets the right mental tone. Your team should be thought of as your total in-house team plus your agency team.

Beyond team size, other types of leverage are often unaccounted for when looking at your agency/services partner:

1. Tech and publisher access — It is very likely that your partner has unique access to the significant partners of the day including but not limited to Google, Meta, Adobe, and Salesforce. There is real economic value here. Understanding the latest feature release in Google could lead to millions of dollars in a positive return on investment, if you can unravel a product mystery via help from these powerful platforms.

2. Insights and knowledge — Every large agency and services company has countless subscriptions to the likes of Kantar, Comscore, Profitero, Nielsen, Forrester, MRI, YouGov, and more. These systems and subscriptions can help you build business cases, create better strategies, or round out a look at a new customer segment. A subscription to any one of these data sources could run you more than $100,000 annually. Make the ask.

3. Thought leadership — The pace of change in the industry is at an all-time high. What will AI mean for your business? What will automation mean for your business? What will be the next social media platform that is material? With an agency, you get access to so many great specialized minds.

Below is a worksheet that might help you consider what value (or lack thereof) you want to consider when analyzing what your partner is bringing to the table.

The point here is simply to recognize the type of leverage you do have via your agency partner and put it to work while being accountable for it.

CONSIDERATION	WHAT TO CONSIDER	VALUE (IN $)
True cost to hire in-house FTEs	Salary, Full Benefits, Travel...	
Technology Access	What is the difference between the DSP (for example) rate your agency gets you versus the higher rate you *might* have yourself	
Negotiated Rates	Your agency might have favored rates with key publishers. Will you miss this advantage?	
Access	Research, Beta Tests, Insights, Expertise	
Hiring Flexibility	Able to more easily move the SOW up or down, or even change the complexion of the team in ways you can't move with internal hires (especially during tougher economic climates)	
Other		
Other		

CHAPTER 16

Be Open to Tough Love from Your Agency Partner

Clients do not fully appreciate it, but it's terrifying for agency partners to provide feedback to them that is tough, controversial, or difficult. Even if the agency client partner is an established professional, it can still be difficult. Why? Well, you the client are paying the bills, in a hyper-competitive market, during a time when relationships are already short. So, when given the choice, the average agency person bites their tongue and resists providing tough-love feedback to a client.

However, to promote a successful partnership from both parties, you want the agency to give feedback. Feedback that comes only from the client limits opportunities for new ideas and real collaboration.

There are two core components for radical candor—caring personally and challenging directly. When giving feedback, using both of those skills is of critical importance. One without the other does not work well.

Terry Griffin was the SVP of Marketing and

Acquisition at Equifax. Terry is a bright, thoughtful, charismatic marketing leader. She hired us with great expectations based on a pitch where we indicated we saw 20%+ opportunity to grow new customers, so she was very much in the right to enter the new engagement with high expectations.

As we started the engagement, we were not at our best. Our forecasts were off. Our results were off. Our reporting had occasional errors. This led Terry to want to dig in, join our daily and weekly calls and ask continued questions. Terry's involvement in the day-to-day inadvertently created a lot of stress and anxiety on the team. I could see their stress as they were now spending 50% of their billable hours preparing for Terry, versus optimizing to get new customers.

So…I took Terry out to lunch at a local restaurant and I spoke to her from the heart. I wanted her to know three core things, one about us and two about her.

1. *"We made you promises during the pitch process that we are right now short of. We will fight every day to do better and earn that trust. We have let you down so far. In that, we have invited extra stress into the engagement."*

With this, I wanted to let her know that the leader on the agency partner side was aware we had not lived up to our commitment.

2. *"You are making the team nervous, which is*

counter-productive, but I sense you don't mean to."

As I got into the heart of the issue, I wanted to be empathic because I was 100% certain it was not intentional. However, she was making the team very nervous.

3. *"You are not giving enough oxygen to your direct reports on your own team, so they are not able to do their job."*

Because we felt paralyzed chasing a forecast, we were also not letting tests find new volume run their course.

To be clear, this was a very difficult meeting to prepare for. There are a lot of industry norms reminding you to just "get along" with your client who pays your bills and your people's mortgages.

Terry, to her credit, took this all incredibly well. Why? Well, all she wanted was for her people to grow, and for her agency to thrive. It also went well because she recognized the two laws of radical candor—directness and passion. This entire episode made Terry a hero to me. She did not care about ego, but rather she cared about winning and getting to a great outcome. She did not care about power dynamics; she cared about improvement. Terry is a true leader.

Terry went on to become a dear friend whom I admire greatly. Most times when we connect on the phone or for a drink, we talk about that meal at

Tavernpointe where I had to deliver "client feedback." It has inspired me to coach others to do the same. Ultimately, clients want to win. Beyond that, most humans want to get better. They might not love what they hear at the moment (don't assume you will get a high five during the feedback), but they will respect you for it later.

CHAPTER 17

Great Clients Can Embrace
Two Opposing Views

One of the things that hurts clients is getting locked in on one view. Having been on the client side twice, I can say from experience I have found myself at times locked in to one view as well. This phenomenon could look something like this:

The client says, "Paid social advertising has never worked for us. The ROI has never been there—let's move on please."

This statement could be highly rational and perhaps rooted in their most immediate experience of not getting ROAS from paid social media. However, it represents a very position-based argument that does not provide a lot of room to hold any other views. Then the agency is forced to defend the other side of the argument which naturally would be, "Well, we know that paid social works for a wide range of clients and you should be open to trying it."

From here, the client holds their belief, and the

agency holds theirs. There is very little room to find creative solutions when this happens. So, where can we turn for a new way forward in this sort of situation?

I draw a lot of inspiration on this topic from Roger Martin's great book, *The Opposable Mind*. The book tells a fairly well-known story of A.G Lafley, who was the new CEO of Procter & Gamble coming in at a time when the stock was down, innovation was failing, and Wall Street was losing confidence.

Lafley was dealing with two very different opinions at P&G. One set of thinking was that Lafley should get back to fiscal responsibility and reign in R&D spending to historical levels at P&G, all within the walls of P&G. The other set of thinking, championed by his predecessor, was to sharply increase R&D and innovation spending to new heights.

To forge a great solution, Lafley decided to grapple with both ideas, trying to find what was right in each of them, while also recognizing how both were insufficient. He did this by questioning assumptions that were made by those who arrived at those very dug-in concepts.

He questioned the reasoning that useful innovation is directly related and proportional to the number of dollars invested into R&D. He asked whether the best R&D would need to happen within the four walls of P&G itself. He looked outside of P&G and discovered that some of the best R&D that was happening was "distributed" amongst think tanks, universities, smaller players, and the like. So, he set a target that P&G would obtain 50% of its innovations from outside of the company by connecting with a wide array of outside innovators. This brought P&G more leverage rather than depending on just his four walls alone. This strategy went on to be titled, "Connect and Develop," which was his way of taking both opposing views within P&G and raising the solution to a better, more nuanced level.

Going back to one of the two dug-in views I put forth earlier, let's look at them one more time through a new lens:

Client says, "Paid social advertising has never worked for us. The ROI has never been there, let's move on please."

Instead, the client should be open to saying, *"We have struggled to make paid social work for us in the past. Maybe the reason for this is how we are evaluating this medium. Perhaps it's because we never had the right targeting or creative approach. I am open to trying this channel again but am looking to find new ways in. Find us a new way in!"*

In short, a great leader does not try to split the middle between two ideas. That is the boring version of compromise. Instead, look for a new middle idea inspired by both ideas on the ends. A better and new idea. A new way to measure. A new way to fund. A new way to give something more time to work or to fail. Great clients can wrestle with conflicting thoughts and help a great agency forge a new path and approach together.

CHAPTER 18

Great Clients Win with Kindness

In 2022, I ran a LinkedIn poll posing the question, "What motivates you to work hard for a client?" Out of 1,005 responses, the top response was "kindness."

As I followed up via direct message with some of the respondents and did my own research, the overwhelming and profoundly simple theme was, "I will absolutely work harder for a client that shows kindness and energy towards our team." While this seems very simple, it's rarer than you might guess.

If you are reading this, it's not likely that you need "kindness lessons," but rather, a kindness why! The why is simple. Agencies are filled with humans, not gearboxes or assembly lines. Humans work at different velocities and different rates based on inspiration. What I have found is that a great client is able to create a virtuous cycle that reinforces confidence, candor, and ultimately great work. It goes something like this:

1. The client delivers briefs and challenges with clarity, enthusiasm, and a feeling that everyone can win together.

2. The agency responds to the challenge with excitement, candor, and optimism.

3. The agency hits deadlines, demonstrates critical thinking, and shares work. In this, the agency demonstrates a positive "Do:Say ratio." In other words, the agency builds confidence in the eye of the client by doing what they said they would do.

4. The client loves the work and shows excitement, gratitude, and appreciation. Or the client does not love the work, still shows gratitude, and then gives clarity as to how it can get better.

5. The agency takes feedback non-defensively, goes back to work, comes back to the client, and shows improvement, as well as their ability to listen and adapt.

6. The client acknowledges the changes, shows gratitude and excitement, and specifically acknowledges that feedback was taken into account.

7. The agency team feels proud as heck and barely remembers they stayed late for a few weeks eating takeout.

What really gets interesting is that the above cycle starts to reinforce a second virtuous cycle, as other great things start to happen:

1. Team retention stays high.

2. The best agency talent begs to get on the train.

3. Awards are won and pride grows.

4. Intimacy grows as the agency feels even more like part of the team.

You can see here that kindness becomes not just a moral imperative (i.e. it's good to follow the golden rule and be kind), but it drives an economic benefit. When you make your agency team feel cared for, human, and part of your team, retention goes up, ideas get better, and overall they dig deeper.

A client's biggest, cheapest, and easiest weapon is kindness. The average agency person is treated very badly from when they break into the business to the day when they retire. It's a hazard of the job that sometimes gets accepted, even though it's not right or fair. This means that the low industry standards of "accepted behaviors" can be used to your advantage! If you can exhibit kindness, and exhibit the most reasonable interpretation (MRI), you can generate your own virtuous cycle with your agency partners.

CHAPTER 19

The Perils of Overplanning

In September of 1862, the Civil War was escalating and its largest battle yet was about to be fought. The Battle of Antietam would be waged between General Robert E. Lee of the South and George McClellan of the North.

Days before the battle was set to commence, two of McClellan's soldiers came across a copy of Lee's detailed battle plans which called for him to divide up his smaller force of 55,000 soldiers (the North had 75,000 in the area) into two distinct forces. McClellan, however, who was the salutatorian at West Point and a known planner, spent the next two days pouring over details and second-guessing things. By this point, Lee had re-consolidated his forces. This allowed him to reduce his losses to the North and retreat to Virginia.

The point of the story, which Scott Sonenshein skillfully shares in his book *Stretch*, referenced in Chapter 11, is that overplanning can have consequences. There has to be muscle memory built in to have a plan that can be adaptive. McClellan had the opportunity to crush the Southern army and change the course of the Civil War, but he was too entrenched in his own plan. He hesitated. He did not have the mindset to take advantage of new information and strike decisively.

As a disclaimer, in no way am I equating marketing to the Civil War or comparing ad strategies to the deadliest battle on U.S. soil. This story, however, is instructive because too often I have seen teams create a very rigid annual marketing plan that makes it nearly impossible to take advantage of the present. Great brands and great marketers have the ability to take advantage of what they see in culture or how they need to pivot to react to competition. To do that, you must have some dry powder as well as the ability to be open to seeing that opportunity. You also need to condition your partner ecosystem to know how to be opportunistic (this is the key!). A simple example of this might be how you approach budgeting with your partner.

One potential exercise to help condition your partner is to use the Now/New/Next framework. Clients get a lot out of agencies when they provide a Now/New/Next framework (see the illustration that follows). I have seen this delivered in a way where budgets are thus distributed. Pretend a client has a budget of $10 million. This might be planned in a way where $6 million goes to immediate priorities of the day. That will be your hardest-working investment. It often needs to see an immediate return associated with it.

Then $3 million might go towards what might be reasonable to focus on tomorrow. This might be new partnership ideas, new advancements, or new targeting techniques. These are small risks and the intention is to apply new learning.

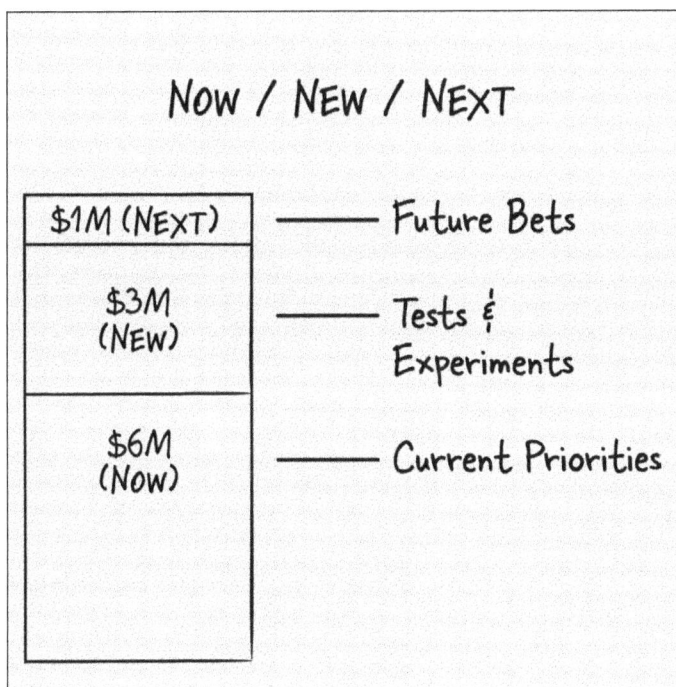

Now / New / Next

$1M (NEXT)	—— Future Bets
$3M (NEW)	—— Tests & Experiments
$6M (NOW)	—— Current Priorities

Finally, $1 million would go into what is next or the equivalent of radical-testing budgets. This "next" category is meant to truly test unique and less-proven ideas. This is where brands go for big rewards, but lower odds of success that come with it. This might also be where brands test still unproven technologies. The idea for clients to understand here is that the precise allocation matters far less than the motivation this method provides. What this says to an agency is "we support trying new things." When the agency hears this, they run with passion to find new ideas for you, the client. Think of this framework as an invitation to your agency partner to reach for the stars versus only thinking about the practical tomorrow.

The modern way of planning is not to be fully planned. Great client-agency relationships will be marked by a move towards agile planning and opportunity funds. As a client, you drive opportunistic behavior when you signal to your agency team there is both a budget and mental room to try and do something new and bold. Don't worry, signaling there is a "next" budget does not mean you are guaranteeing anything, but rather that you are open to something great should they bring you that opportunity.

Showing your agency you are open to greatness ... is how you get greatness.

CHAPTER 20

Always Set the Standard

There is an underrated and little-known job that the best clients perform. The best clients know how to subtly and consistently set the standard for the agency team. Through repetition, a great client is able to remind an agency at every turn what matters most to the client, company, and brand.

An agency by nature is a creative, idea-generating organism. It will always try to come up with new ideas, new ways in, and new concepts. Each new idea could be great, but it just as easily could go off course. In this way, job number one for a client is to keep the agency aware of the standard. A great client reminds the agency what the brand stands for, why the company does what it does, and what the core values are.

Danny Meyer, a famous New York City restaurant owner, writes in his book *Setting the Table* about how to run an amazing restaurant steeped in customer service. In a sense, his core thesis is that the general manager of a restaurant must constantly remind the entire staff, in the most consistent and not-so-subtle ways, what the bar is.

In one of the chapters, he talks about the lesson Pat Cetta gave him and how he now uses that to train all his wait staff and general managers. Employing Cetta's lesson, he stares at one of the tables that is set and asks the staff member to take everything off the table except the salt. So, the waiter goes ahead and removes the plates, the glassware, the cutlery, and everything else. Danny then asks the waiter if he feels like the saltshaker is in the middle of the table.

The waiter responds that he indeed feels it is. Danny inspects the table in detail and then teaches the waiter that the saltshaker was actually one-quarter inch off from the center.

He goes on to explain, "Your guests are always moving your saltshaker off center. That is their job. Unless you understand that, you will get upset. It's not your job to get upset. Your job is to move the shaker back each time and let them know exactly what you stand for. Let them know what excellence looks like to you."

What does this story have to do with you as a client? Your main role is to help an agency continue to do the following:

- understand the standard
- understand what great is

- understand why that standard is so important
- remind them over and over and over again what the brand is about

The greatest clients set this standard in a motivational way, focused on the brand, and focused on learning together. When you move the saltshaker back to the center, it helps the agency stay centered. Great partnerships allow for this healthy back and forth.

CONCLUSION

The concept of being a great client is one that felt a bit daunting to write. I worried that I could seem preachy. I worried the book could feel biased. I worried that it could be taken the wrong way. In the end, if you can write purely from the heart on a topic, then you should just be brave and do it. The purity here comes from my own experiences and talks with my client-side friends that there is a true need for training around this topic.

Every agency is made up of humans. These humans have a lot to do in a given day, and money and fear are not motivators that work on a longitudinal basis. The best ideas flock to the best clients. The best team members flock to the best clients. The greatest velocity of work gravitates toward the best clients. The best and most thoughtfully written contracts and staffing models create the best work for clients.

The clients who create personal relationships with their agency partners will get the most passion aimed back at them and their business. The clients who lead with kindness and the most reasonable interpretation (MRI) get agency teams who are brave and willing to try and experiment because they don't fear reprisal. The clients who take time to contextualize how their business works, and where advertising and marketing rest within that broader context, get agencies who are therefore smarter and are now armed with more holistic and informed thinking.

All of this could seem extra credit behavior, right? Well, the purpose of this book is to point out how this sort of behavior can not only set you apart but allow you to get more value out of your agency relationships.

Surprise your agency partner today. You won't just bring a smile to their faces if you deploy tactics from a few of these chapters. More so, I promise you will drive huge value for yourself, your team, your brand, and your customers.

ACKNOWLEDGMENTS

So many of the lessons in this book exist only because I have gotten to watch some of the most incredible clients (whom I count as friends) nurture relationships with agencies and inspire. I want to thank all our past and current clients at Acadia for trusting us.

Thanks to the team at Ripples Media (Jaye Liptak, Andrew Vogel, Jeff Hilimire, and Rachelle Kuramoto) for nurturing this book along the way. It is a niche topic for sure, but you believed in me and found ways big and little to show how much you cared.

I want to thank my wife Jeanine who always believes in me and supports me to take time to write and think. She is a great client partner in her own right and helped me bounce around all sorts of ideas.

I also have to thank the two best kids a dad could ask for in Avner and Alex. They are curious, thoughtful, smart, interesting, and kind. My parents, cousins, friends, and co-workers continue to always be there for me, and I am the luckiest guy because of it. One day, I promise to return texts or calls at a faster pace.

I am able to put something back into this industry only because so many have invested in me. I am thankful every day to the number of people who reach out or respond with help and advice. Go do the same with someone else. The world is better with more teachers.

ABOUT THE AUTHOR

Jared Belsky is CEO and Co-Founder of Acadia, a powerhouse digital marketing and analytics agency.

Before co-founding Acadia with Sean Belnick, Jared was CEO of 360i, one of the top advertising and marketing agencies in the U.S. Under Jared's leadership, 360i was named *Adweek*'s Breakthrough Media Agency of the year, repeatedly ranked among the best Performance Marketing Agencies by Forrester research, and featured in *AdAge*'s coveted A-List issue for eight consecutive years.

He is also the author of *The Great Client Partner*,

written to help educate and inspire around soft skills, and is a frequent contributor to *AdAge*, *Adweek*, and *AdExchanger*.

Over his career, he has been honored as one of the industry's top leaders. He was named to the Class of 2023 by Campaign 40 Over 40, recognizing individuals for groundbreaking work and outside-the-box thinking. Previously, he has been named to *AdAge*'s "40 Under 40" in 2017, honored as Executive of the Year at the 2016 Bing Agency Awards, and was the only person named in back-to-back years to *Adweek*'s Media All-Star list in 2014 and again in 2015.

Jared is an active member of the Atlanta investment and entrepreneurial community. Jared serves as an Operating Partner for Overline, is on the board of directors for direct-to-consumer laundry start-up 2ULaundry, and gives back to Emory as a board member for EIG (Emory's Impact Investment Group), which aims to close the financing gap through short-term investments to entrepreneurs in the Atlanta community.

Before Acadia and 360i, Jared had over a decade of digital marketing experience, including launching a new CPG brand, managing the integrated media budget for Coca-Cola's Fanta brand, and working in media buying and account roles as one of the first employees at Avenue A (now Sapient Razorfish).

Jared received an MBA from Emory University in

Marketing and Management and a BA with Honors from the University of Pennsylvania. When not working, Jared is with family and close friends. He enjoys time in nature—ideally, Acadia National Park. If not that, he can be seen rooting for the Mets (which creates a lot of resilience) or figuring out his lifelong dream of being a college professor one day, 15 years from now.

ABOUT *THE GREAT CLIENT PARTNER*

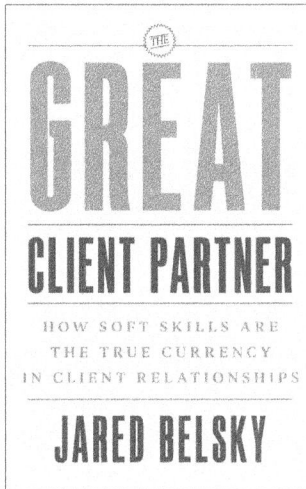

There's no such thing as a "natural born leader."

In Jared Belsky's first book, he explains how great leaders have a set of abilities essential to working with and inspiring others, including trust building, persuasion, time management, principled negotiating, and active listening. All of these soft skills can be learned, and Belsky details exactly how to pick up and internalize them.

The Great Client Partner is your guide to honing your

soft skills to complement your technical expertise, making you ready to lead large teams, innovate, and build trust with your clients and internal and external stakeholders. When you master this rare combination of hard and soft skills, there's no limit to how far your career can go.

This book is your key to successful client relationships and incredible upward career mobility.

OTHER TITLES FROM RIPPLES MEDIA

The 5-Day Turnaround

The Crisis Turnaround

The Great Team Turnaround

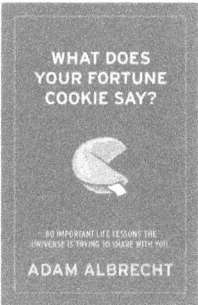

What Does Your Fortune Cookie Say?

6Ps of Essential Innovation

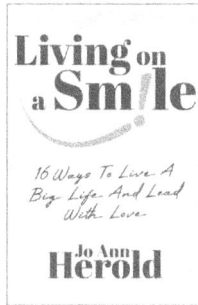

Living on a Smile

The Culture Turnaround

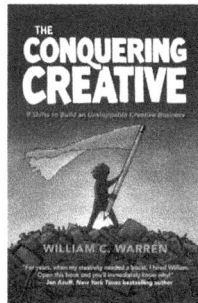

The Conquering Creative

www.ingramcontent.com/pod-product-compliance
Lightning Source LLC
Chambersburg PA
CBHW040928210326
41597CB00030B/5215